These poems have been written out of a series of (pro)found (a)wakenings & experiences i had (re)turning from a three year journey, studying yoga & starting a family in Mexico.

In the following years, (re)flecting on my experiences and learning, i (dis)covered an (i)ronic & poetic link between the life lessons i was (re)ceiving & the language i was using to (de)scribe them.
These pages are filled with my dreams, visions & (re)flections that i feel can gently (ar)ticulate many of the (pro)cesses one goes through in this journey of waking up.

As you may see, i am using brackets to highlight (pre)fixes. For (re)ference, in styles, (an)ything in a bracket is not considered on the page. These (pre)fixes i have learnt, create a (ne)gative condition of state, to the root meanings of the words. Any word beginning with a vowel & two consonants (ne)gates the root word, as does any word beginning with a one syllable vowel.

As you read through this book you will find many surprising (re)velations, not only (a)bout language but also (a)bout numbers, law & wisdom teachings that have been woven into riddles & rhyme.
I wish through these pages, to (en)tertain, (e)ducate, (en)lighten and (in)spire the reader, to the wonder & magic, both light & dark, in this crazy world we live in, in the trust that you too can wake up to the knowing that you & everything about these (ex)pereinces we have here, are divine.

May these poems untether the spells cast on us through the modification of the English language. May these poems (re)mind us of our greatness & may these poems sweetly (re)vive the playfulness of the (in)ner child, that we each hold within.
This is my wish & gift to you.

Bolon Ik.

♥

To Uma Sophia & Gaia Regina you are Gifts from God sent to bless
my life with your (pre)sence.
Papa will be home soon... Los amo!

Mis Amores,
los Amo.
Estan en Mexico,
Estoy en oltra Mundo.
Uma estas mi Galactica,
Y Gaia estas mi Tierra.
Estan mi Vida,
En Unidad...
Es verdad!

♥

Contents

Hermetics

The Law of Mentalism + The Law of Correspondence +
The Law of Vibration + The Law of Polarity + The Law of Rhythm +
The Law of Cause & Effect + The Law of Gender

(An)tiquity

Brothers & Sisters + The Hero's Journey + His-story + Way Out West
+ Footsteps & Shoulders + Syncretism +
Question what to believe

Magic Spelling

These words Symbols & Signs + Words Of Wisdom + Fiction To Fact
+ If You Have The Eyes To See + (In)ner Library + The Magic Of A
Roundabout + What Is A (De)finition + To Write (A)bout + (Ne)gation +
I AM-The One + For The Claim Of The Life + Etymology +
1+2=3=Me+You=We + The Wisdom Of The Word + The Secret In
Numbers + Path Of Least Resistance + The Poet Be-Comes The
Poem + Who's Scribbled The Script + The Clues To Get Out Of This
Mess + Lingustic Prison

New Earth

Daughters & Sons + Our Playground + Walk With Me
+ (In)ner Guru + The Great Uplifting + Transformational Force + I AM +
Where We Go One We Go All + (In)tervention

Family

Divine (Or)der + 8.8.8 + The Great (Ad)venture + Can You See? +
My Family Of Magic & Wonder + Where Do We Go From Here? +
The Time Has Come + My Babies I Love You + Sweet Uma & Gaia +
Oh Grief + Goodbye Sadness + Dear Tara

(In)ner Child

Child's Play

Today is the day,
Life becomes child play,
To hear what i'm gonna say
(An-o)ther way.
It's (a)bout those good vibes.
The coming of the tides,
No one be ostracized,
In this day 'n age.
The rainbow tribe is here,
To guide & steer,
Humanity,
To a place without fear.
I plant a seed in you,
A flower as sacred as sage.
Those old beliefs have now faded with age,
(Ac)cept what you may,
Everything is okay,
I've done things Marilyn Manson can claim to say!
In love we are made,
Luminating the shade,
The (in)ner child we lost,
Now comes out to play.

♥

Game Boy

I grew up with Transformers,
And (En)gland footballers,
Singing New order's song.
With Michael Jackson moonwalking,
Home (a)lone with Macaulay Culkin,
Did he really do something wrong?
Arnold Schwarzenegger in Terminator,
Morning TV with Mr Motivator,
Was this in me,
Could i really be strong?
With all these (re)flections,
of my childhood fascinations,
I was a Game Boy,
Playing on Donkey Kong.

♥

A Place I know

Today i went to a place i know,
To bark on a great new venture.
With some help from the crew,
I was up high with a view,
To let go of my fears & surrender.
Today i faced the dragon of St. Lenord,
With open arms & open-hearted.
With the magic of a potion,
I am free from all notions,
To dream a new dream (en)chanted.
Today i (re)member (e)ternal youth,
In a way that was very surprising.
All that i see,
Now (re)flects to me,
The trooth in its many (dis)guises.

♥

Microtia

When i was young...
I would love to run,
To the shops and back with a snack.
When I was young...
Summers were fun,
Playing football out late with my mates.
When i was young...
Holidays in the Sun,
were (ad)ventures i'll always (re)member.
Now i am older..
Watching Scully & Mulder,
On the x-files i see microtia.
To the surprise of my eyes,
(An)swers to my questions why,
Is of alien DNA from the skies?

♥

I AM God

Don't be (a)fraid to lose yourself,
Cause your more than you've ever dreamed.
In fact i'd go as far to say,
You've created everything you've ever seen!
And now you know your everything,
The state of the game has changed.
With a blink of an eye,
You'll be up in the sky,
Saying, I AM God..
And i can fly!

♥

I Have A Dream

I have a dream..
where we are all free,
Living our lives,
In peace & harmony.

I have a dream..
where we know who we are,
Spiritual beings,
Creators of the stars.

I have a dream..
where we know the trooth,
we are all one,
with the (in)nocence of youth.

I have a dream..
where mysteries are solved,
with children so wise,
They never grow old.

I have a dream..
where lands are lush & green,
vibrant & clean,
Free from poverty...

I have a dream..
of global (un)ity,
The (up)liftment of all,
In a bundance & (e)quality.

I have a dream..
of (in)terstellar ET's,
who help us (per)ceive,
we're part of a galactic family.

I have a dream...
of a beautiful queen bee,
who saves humanity,
And my dreams be-come reality.

♥

Masculine & Feminine

To honor the feminine,
we must first face our gremlins,
we might not realize are there.
The old system of patriarchy,
where men be-came nasty,
And forget to be gentle and care.
With all this conditioning,
Compassionate hearts are listening,
To the (in)ner child,
who was lost and scared.
And when we (re)concile,
with the hate and the vile,
we can honour the women,
In style....
Now for the masculine,
who forget they're half feminine,
In the balance of yin and yang...
Many are threatening,
with violence that's sentencing..
People to shelter in gangs.
To end the patriarchy,
we must (re)member the vulnerability,
of the masculine way to play.
And when this is done,
The conflict is won,
we (a)scend through a portal we call the Sun.

♥

Forever Ever Land

You are an (ex)pression,
of The one (in)finite Creator,
You are your maker.
A wolf in sheep's clothing,
King of the dogs.
Dog is God spelt backwards,
This system's fractured.
Your Clark Kent & Superman,
Get it!?
You and every person can,
So start playing with some mighty plans,
God knows,
Produce dope music with Timberland,
And live like Peter Pan,
In forever ever land.

♥

The Landings

My (re)flections are packed,
In a 90's dance track,
That timely plays its tune.
I feel my heart (ex)panding
As we (pre)pare for the landings,
In 2022!

♥

Galactic Family

When i look up at the sky tonight,
I see planets and stars,
(A)ligned,
(A)light.
And as i look up,
In wonder and awe,
I see beings look back at me,
More and more.
We are part of a galactic family.
We forgot..
(Re)member our story.
So now we are ready and ripe,
To join them in sheer (de)light.
Cause finally we are home,
In a higher dimensional zone,
We be-come one,
With no need for our phones!

♥

Expressions of God

What will change your mind,
For your life is the same as mine.
Some people may call it God.
And you can see it in a dog.
While (o)thers can look to the stars,
To know they are one..
With the body of Mars.
So never forget,
A wonderful pet,
Is a beautiful (ex)pression of God.

♥

Crystal Magic

These crystals,
They smell like magic.
So many don't see it,
It's tragic!
With colours so bright,
Luminating their light,
(Re)leasing the might of tektite.

♥

Now I see The Picture

These cosmic (ac)tivations,
(A)waken the force,
Of Love & (under)standing,
For I Am One with Source.
Childhood memories,
Of stirred (e)motions,
In songs i can see,
A heart closed and broken.
Now with (re)flection,
I can see the reason,
In metaphors & lyrics,
Of George Michael's song Freedom.
So many signs..
Now i see the picture,
Of the messages being said,
By starseeds in scripture.
I Am the dreamer,
Of these pieces of art,
And in my dream,
They waken my Heart.

❤

Child Like

I felt like a child (a)gain tonight,
Going to sleep alone in bed.
Surrounded by toys,
My heart filled with joy
To (re)member the (in)nocence,
of being a...
Three year old boy.

♥

Heaven & Earth

Heaven & Earth,
Are (u)ntied at birth,
(U)pon your very (ar)rival.
Your Mum & your Pops
who do love you lots,
Looked after you for your survival.
As you grew up,
And sometimes felt stuck,
It was all part of the learning.
Allow the tears to flow,
Through these lessons we grow,
The cycles of Life forever turning.
The wisdom of age,
Is what is (a)live on this page,
So be grateful & make sure you enjoy it.
For you are also forever young,
A Starchild of the Sun,
who came to (U)nite Heaven & Earth,
For fun.

♥

Living The Dream

In one year from now,
By the 8th of August,
I plan to (ex)perience the top.
I see myself playing,
on a Spider dj-ing,
with one of my heroes,
Carl Cox!
In (A)valon it will be,
where we change his-story,
Through the love,
of this heart frequency.
As we (a)lign with this solstice,
Gaia celebrates a new Earth shift,
We be-come one,
Trust me,
We're not Faithless!
Is that God up there?
A galactic human,
I swear.
And now we're all blissed out,
In Christ consciousness!

♥

Nature

We Are All One

You are one with all that is.
That (in)cludes...
The birds and the trees and the seas,
And the giraffe that laughs in the grass.
As well as the planets, their (o)ceans and motions,
You are the neutrons, electrons and protons.
With this in mind..
I'll say it one more time.
Your Heart is the same as mine!!

♥

Animal Totem

What's the meaning of a spider,
That crawls up (be)side ya,
In symbol & metaphor?
When we search for the trooth,
Life will give us the proof,
That Life is a (re)flection,
For sure!
So when a Eagle flies low,
We have the tools to know,
What the mirror is saying,
At its core.
Keep those eyes to the skies,
And keep asking why,
To watch your Consciousness,
Fly forever more.

♥

Little Bird Big Tree

I hear a beautiful song,
By a little bird,
In a big tree.
That grew from a tiny wee seed.
(re)member..
It doesn't matter what your size is,
It's whats (in)side that's surprising.
So don't judge a book by it's cover,
There's some treasure in here to (dis)cover.

♥

The Essence of A Tree

The archetypal energy,
of a tree,
Is stability,
So hug them,
And feel their majesty.
As their roots,
Bed down in solidity,
They are (es)tablished,
And grow (in-de)pendently.
They stand tall,
And gracefully,
(A)mongst their friends,
And family.
Showing their strength,
over (ad)versity,
Baring their fruits
(a)bundantly,
And dropping their leaves,
(In)sularity
To reflect our gifts,
And Potentiality.

♥

Sound

Vibrations the tone,
(Re)lated to depth,
I (re)cognize in sound.
The frequency pitch,
Carries the height,
These are the aspects of sound i found.
So what (a)bout width,
And how it transmits,
In a dimension that's been soncially drowned.
So let's (re)discover,
The truth of the lover,
Who creates this creation through sound.

♥

Water

As we structure the water,
It gives us its life,
Now it's full of Toruses.
Geometrically formed,
(In)tentionally transformed,
So we are healed from all of our viruses.

♥

Circles & Cycles

Cycles are All There Is,
Eons of cycles of this.
Rotating circles of tor,
Spiralling patterns in form.
Cycles are All There Is,
(Under)standing these cycles of time,
With circles & geometrical lines,
And Mayan calendar (de)signs.
The wheel of God is All There Is,
Ask the Zodiac astrologist,
The one- sided shape,
Many (re)late,
To the (U)nion of All That Is.

♥

Grandfather Fire

Grandfather Fire,
Torch these beastly (de)sires,
To purify this soul (a)new.
On this full moon of twins,
I bare my shadows to you,
(Ex)ercising the past i (on)ce knew.
Burning this house,
Old structures deloused,
As a rainbow wave ablaze.
My fears become fuel,
To flame freedom for all,
Sovereign beings step out of the shade.
Great spirit (ig)nite,
The light of the heart,
In this soul's darkest nights.

♥

Bitter & Sweet

A mango tree,
For months of the year,
Out of season the leaves,
Taste bitter you hear.
(A)long comes April,
The moment of spring,
As the mangos ripen,
With sweetness fit for a King.

♥

Love

Now I Know What Love Is

Now i know what love is,
I am Free.
Now i know what love is,
I can see.

Do not fear my dear,
For things are not (al)ways how they (ap)pear..
You are love,
You are the night,
And you are the light.

In our hearts there is a space..
Of (e)ternal knowing,
Glowing (il)lumination within,
A sea of bliss not sin.

Look with the eyes of trooth,
To know what love is,
And you will see,
You are forever free.

♥

Love Liberates

Love liberates...
In times of heartache,
Through compassionate actions You make.
Trust luminates...
The depths of your soul,
The past,
Let it go,
It's so old!
Honesty (in)spires...
The ones who are liars,
To speak the Trooth and (en)quire.
Generosity (am)plifies...
(E)motions that make us cry,
Now the Love vibration is magnified.
Pure (in)tention (ex)presses...
To the Gods and Goddesses,
Your heart is (a)ligned with The Divine...
Joy (u)nifies...
The Earth and the skies,
So now the E.T.'s can say hi!
Forgiveness penetrates...
The (in)evitable (mis)takes,
To realize Christ consciousness states.
And wisdom (e)vaporates...
The (i)dea of fear,
For you are Great Spirit,
In the colour of a blue deer.

♥

Love Virus

Code name...
Love Virus.
The mission...
To (in)fect Miley Cyrus,
And the masses,
with a vision of (U)topian living.
It's time to (U)nite,
To jump and take flight,
To break free from this old corrupt system.
007 we play..
Hacking the system the Taoist way,
'Cause did you know...
Love is the transformative force.
So (em)brace the fear
And see it so clear..
Your in love with the Love Virus,
You hear me cheer!

♥

Love is...

Two people holding hands,
On bicycles in (Am)sterdam.
Warm breakfast croissants,
With butter & jam.
Love is...
(Ad)miring Life's sacred creations,
Riding past Central Station.
Through this city maze,
In Liberty's haze.
Love is...
Hot chocolate & cream,
So cold outside it steams,
By the canals,
This place is Heaven,
House 111.
Love is...
Dancing in the temple of Solomon,
Who's wisdom has created a following,
A feeling of being born again!
Triangle shapes are (or)biting.
At a Rainbow tribe gathering,
I'm high now..
Thanks to Dom Perignon!

♥

The (E)ternal force

This world is full of magic,
Mystery, folklore and grace.
Love is the (e)ternal force,
of (in)ner and outer space.

♥

The hand of God

I was touched by the hand of God tonight,
It was the purest thing i've ever seen.
I took a ride on a (U)nicorn,
To places i've (al)ways dreamed.
Tonight i touched an (an)gel,
If only she could see,
We were blessed by God tonight,
And forever may we be.

♥

Rainbow Love

Last night i drew a rainbow,
Fueled by the love (in)side of me.
On a wall,
within a flower,
The colours are bright to see.
Last night in rainbow cottage,
I (o)pened to (e)ternity,
Resting forever,
In the love that sets us free.

♥

what if..

what if love is all you need..
would you love to be free?
what if love is all there is..
would you love it all & forgive?
what if love is the cure to heal..
would you love this to be real?
what if love is who you are..
would you love your deepest scars?
what if love is the reason we (ex)ist..
would you love the pain you (re)sist?
what if love is the way to be..
would you love what i say & (ag)ree?
what if love is an (e)ternal force..
would you love & (ac)cept this is Source?
what if love is this poem you read,
would you love this flowering seed?
what if this love in me is in you..
would you love this to be true?

♥

(U)nion of Souls

Today we gather,
Lovers in redwoods,
To celebrate a (u)nion of souls.
(Re)member the force,
Said by Yoda of course,
Sealed with a kiss,
This bond is so bold.
So forget what you were told,
This wisdom is so old.
We witness true love,
And I am sold!

♥

Love Will Set Us Free

On the date of 8.8.8.
Known as the Lion's Gate,
I found peace (in)side of me,
Love flowed out for (e)ternity.
I knew then we can never be [a]part,
And that love will set us free.
The love that i am,
Is the love that you are,
So listen carefully,
Your heart is a star.
Shining to galaxies near & far,
Your love is all there is,
So realize the trooth,
You are The one..
The only one ever to (ex)ist.

♥

Let's Close Our Eyes

Let's close our eyes in bed tonight,
And let us feel what happens.
Let me touch you softly,
All over your temple-body.

(Re)member to keep your eyes closed,
And be open to receive,
Close your eyes sweet heart,
You're safe here with me.

Let's close our eyes in bed tonight,
Come on a journey with me,
My kiss is so tender,
You'll be filled with (ec)stasy.

Keep your eyes closed now,
It's better not to see,
You feel so much deeper,
And taste so much sweeter,
Cause your other senses (in)crease.

Don't open your eyes yet,
There's so much more you can see,
When you come (in)side with me,
You will find where heaven be.

Keep those eyes closed now,
It's more (ex)citing not to see.
We're going on a venture,
To our wildest fantasies.

♥

The Love In You

This love is so pure and true,
Most people have not a clue.
If you stay up late,
To learn to meditate.
You can find this love..
That's in you.

♥

The Indian Boy

one night..
God came to visit me,
In the shape of a Indian boy.
He took one loving look at me,
And my heart burst into joy!

♥

The Indian Boy Pt.2

In my darkest days,
(A)lone & broken,
Ramana (ap)peared,
In silence spoken,
And in that moment,
Something (o)pened,
This tender heart,
To love & (de)votion.

♥

The voice of God

Last night i heard the voice of God,
(U)pon the crystal solstice,
At Cadogan hall,
i heard the angels call,
Songs of love & oneness.

♥

A Lovers Story

Rising Sun,
Brilliantly bright,
Everyone,
Is seeing light.
(Morn)ing glory,
A brand new day,
A lovers story,
The nameless way.
Nighttime stars,
A full clear moon,
Seems so far,
We'll be there soon.
(Un)known mysteries,
(In)finite space,
(Re)writing our story,
In cosmic grace.

♥

(A)doration

It was just after we (ar)rived,
I was very surprised,
To see you on the window sill.
I felt the need to get down,
on one knee for you,
And gently kneel.
Your scent is so Heavenly sweet,
I can feel it in my feet.
I'm so happy we've had the chance to meet.
I want to taste your (in)ner sensations
To me you are a (re)presentation,
of a timelessness (il)lumination.
You're like the Queen in the cattle
Searing kundalini rattle
(Ig)niting the pineal..
The divine pineapple!
May you ripe into a star,
Like the fruit that you are.
As The Sun sets,
At Cafe Del Mar.

♥

You Are Love

You are love,
And you're witnessing your own mental suffering.
Open to the everythingness that you are.
You are love,
So (em)brace of all that suffering,
Because love is what you truly are.
You are love.
Come to terms with who you really are.
You are love.
You have come from the stars
You are love
You're more than the mind can ever be.
You are love.
So let go of that personality..
Because that is not you.
You are love,
Shining your light as the love that you are.

♥

Love & (A)wareness

Realize that this moment contains love,
Constantly see this love in your (a)wareness.
When you see (a)nother being,
Know it's The Creator you are seeing,
'Cause we are all one in consciousness.

♥

Untether The Leather

At one point in the night,
I could feel your fright,
That i was judging you.
You must (re)member,
I'm not a (pre)tender
I love you, (re)member?
Surrender.
In all your confusion,
I found a solution,
For you to trust in me.
I gave you a blessing,
In a way you weren't guessing,
To untether the leather,
Forever.

♥

Finally

"Finally you come (a)round..."
To hear those (a)ligned and sacred sounds.
with its meaning,
I'm beaming.
These words i am singing..
"If you only knew,
How i feel about You".
This Love in me is so true.

♥

Sacred Ceremony

An (an)gel cleansed my soul tonight,
with her feathered wings,
Together we honour the spirits,
In love & harmony we sing.
Tonight we made an (of)fering,
To be the change we have come here to be,
Tonight we come to-gather..
In prayer of love & (u)nity.

♥

The Heart

Go to your heart,
I will meet you there,
where your dreams are fulfilled,
with love, compassion and care.
Your heart is your home,
A place to feel comfortable,
welcoming (o)thers,
A space to feel vulnerable.
So trust in your heart,
And the rhythms of life,
As it guides us home,
To a life without strife.
Earth is our playground,
A school of (re)membering,
And the heart is our tool,
we (re)member to surrender in.

♥

My Muse

when your ready,
we will be together.
I know it in my heart.
Together forever,
May we (re)member,
That death can not keep us (a)part

♥

wisdom of (Re)flection

Life Is A Riddle

Life is a riddle,
wrapped in mystery,
(In)side of an (e)nigma,
Living in synchronicity.

♥

Say Yes

This life,
we take it so serious,
Yet the trooth is far more mysterious.
If we can learn to let go,
And stop saying no,
we can play & dance,
And Life can flow.
So when we say no,
To things we don't know,
we close ourselves to new possibilities.
And when we say yes,
To life,
we are blessed,
with new ventures and (op)portunities.

♥

Clear Vision

Like a blind man who now has clear vision,
I'm free from the labels of ism's.
This life is simply a dream,
Like a movie,
And I'm the star of the screen.
I'm the wise one who gives you the keys,
To unlock the mind & its (be)liefs.
So (en)quire with what you (be)lieve..
And know you can succeed,
To do something good for humanity.

♥

No Separation

As i rise from my dream,
I look to you,
As a source of Love and (in)spiration.
Don't be a stranger,
There is no danger,
In this (be)lief of separation.
I know I am you.
Do you know it too,
This path of self-realization.

♥

(A)wareness

So now let's talk about (a)wareness.
For most people's (at)tention is careless.
I'm here on a mission,
To (ac)knowledge and listen,
To the witness of my own mental prison.
It's taken some time,
For these concepts to (a)lign,
To new levels of life and (in)nerstanding.
When we listen to our mind,
We sense something deep (in)side,
Through self (e)nquiry,
This (pre)sence becomes (ac)tualized.

♥

(In)tention

When you learn about this thing called (in)tention,
You will see it's a beautiful (re)flection,
In the world i guarantee.
To change what you say,
In a more positive and powering way,
Life gets easier,
Day by day.
(On)ce you know it,
You know it,
You can use it,
And prove it,
That your (in)tention can set you free.
And (on)ce that has happened,
You'll be straight outta Clapham,
On a spaceship near Uranus and Saturn!

♥

Transfiguration

There's this thing called transfiguration,
That (re)quires some practice and patience.
When you look in the eyes,
Of a warm and trusted guy,
They become windows to many dimensions.
Try this with your lover,
Your Brother or Mother,
And watch as you (re)cognize each (o)ther.
But not as a person,
A soul,
The same version,
And (re)member we're all one (an-o)ther.

♥

Change

When life gets way too (re)petitive,
Make some changes it's (im)perative.
(A)lign with the rhythms of nature,
To help you balance your behaviour.
(Re)member,
Life never stays the same,
It's your old patterns that's got to change.

♥

The Mirror

The mirror is neutral,
(Re)flecting what it sees.
If i see through the lens of light,
It (re)flects it back to me.
If i judge the world as dark,
It (re)flects it back to be.
The key is to be the mirror,
In complete neutrality.

♥

The Camera of Life

Who looks through the lens,
of the camera of life?
This life you are living is photography.
How you see,
Is a (pro)jection to be,
Life however it is you see it to be.

Who looks through the lens,
of the camera of life?
This life you are living is photography.
What you feel,
(Pro)jects on the reel,
This Life whatever way you feel it to be.

Who looks through the lens,
of the camera of life?
This life you are living is photography.
What you (pro)ject,
Directly (af)fects,
Your Life and how it is you (per)ceive it to be.

Who looks through the lens,
of the camera of life?
This life you are living is photography.
Whatever you love,
Is seen from (a)bove,
As Life and how lovely you love it to be...

As i look through the lens,
of the camera of life,
This life i realize is photography.
As i (e)dit the old memories,
To project a new story,
I change my life and my autobiography.

❤

I Am The Dreamer

I am the dreamer,
Dreaming my dream,
Creating the (ex)perience i see in the scene.
So when i wake up,
I (re)member i make up,
The reality i see,
That's outside of me.
I am the dreamer,
Dreaming my dream,
Creating the (ex)perience i see in this scene.
As i turn off my mind,
where there's nothing to find,
I (re)lax & float down stream.
For i am the dreamer,
Dreaming my dream,
Creating everything that's ever been.

♥

Your Heart

You are the heart of who you are,
You are the heart of what you do.
You're the heart of what you see,
You're the heart of what you (be)lieve.
You're the heart of how you feel,
And you're the heart of how you play.
You're the heart of that star on the screen,
You're the heart of the dream that you dream.

♥

Self-Realization

This dawning of a new civilization,
Is cause for a celebration.
We are the generation..
Who (em)body vulnerability and patience.
So let's heal these wounds,
And be-come (at)tuned,
To the self-realization..
Of creation.

♥

Habitual Patterns

If we could see what our patterns create,
It would make for an (in)teresting picture.
Are your patterns life (af)firming,
or are they more concerning?
If you do not like your patterns,
Create some more beautiful ones,
To (de)sign a life with more fun.
It is your picture your painting,
With these patterns your making,
So (re)member your The Creator creating.

♥

The Shadow

The thing with the shadow is,
Its nature is the darkness,
which can be a difficult place to be.
Look with your light,
To luminate the night,
To see whatever there is you need to see.
You might find a treasure,
That's worth your (en)deavor,
(A)bout your past & the story of your family.
So look at the stuff you hide (a)way,
It will have some (be)neficial things it wants to say.

♥

Little Big Voice

You are listening to your (un)conscious mind,
That little big voice in your head.
It's not who you are,
Your the one who (in)habits the stars,
So feed your multi-dimensionality (in)stead!

♥

The Ego

The ego loves to play a game,
The game of right or wrong.
Let go of these views,
(Em)brace the heart of your muse,
To realize you're one with the trooth.

♥

Yoga

When you don't practice yoga,
Your body feels older,
(Un)able to stretch and function.

So always (re)member,
To help you stay stronger,
With this practice..
You live longer and longer.

To look at a Yantra,
Or sing a favourite Mantra,
You tap into the source of creation.

This energy some can see it,
If you're still you might just feel it,
In Yoga it's called a (re)velation.

❤

Before You were Born

These (ex)periences we have are not random.
When you wake up,
You realize you planned 'em.
Before you were born,
And your clothes were worn..
You are a soul,
who can never grow old.

♥

(Re)flections

This world is a (re)flection of me,
And (on)ce you see it,
It's mastery.
So when you're feeling low,
Life will show you so.
And when you're feeling great,
That love will (re)plicate!
You are looking in a mirror my dear.
So love what you see..
The mystery,
Even the misery..
To know (in)finity!

♥

The veil

When people see planes,
Many complain about that noise..
And those chemtrails.
Yet for me..
I see people,
Flying high in the sky.
With this (per)ception we can see through the veil.

♥

SatChitAnanda

As consciousness..
You are (a)wareness..
which is pure (ex)istence..
which means everlasting (ex)perience...
Your are pure bliss,
which manifest as (en)ergy..
That is love at its (es)sence...
which is Life itself.
You are Gods & Goddesses...
Sacred & divine..
By living through the heart..
You live in deathless oneness..
The same as Jesus Christ consciousness!

♥

The Gift of (In)tuition

The path of our learning,
Is carved in the (pre)sent moment,
if only you'd (re)cognize.
Take time to listen,
To that gift called (in)tuition,
You're making your movie..
So fantasize.

♥

(Dis)tillation

I am a Starseed,
Who learnt sacred geometry,
The Tao & the nameless way.
To know the perfection,
In Life & it's (re)flections,
Is the game i play today.
The people i meet,
Are so loving & sweet,
A mirror of me i say.
So start living your dream,
(Dis)tilling water from steam,
Is the transformative way to play.

♥

The watcher

I Am picking & (un)tangling,
The (dis)tortions of reality,
Through the (re)flections of the world (a)round me.
The beings in front of me,
And the thoughts inside me,
Show me the trooth in all its Glory.

♥

one by one

You're a mirror of me,
Can you see,
In all your different sizes.?
When you know how to be,
You'll be (e)ternally free,
One by one humanity rises.

♥

Who Am I?

Who Am I?
I thought i knew,
Someone true,
Yet these thoughts are as concrete as sky.

Who Am I,
without these (be)liefs,
(im)planted motifs,
To be passive & (al)ways comply?

Who Am I,
when i don't get my way,
or like what you say?
What are these fellings i'm feeling (in)side?

Who Am I
In these testing moments,
Facing (op)ponents,
Who love to crucify?

Who Am I,
when i face my past?
These old masks now crumbling fast,
I AM... Now i'm ready to fly!

♥

(U)nique (Per)spective

Don't lose yourself to be (ac)cepted,
To an (i)dea you (on)ce (re)jected,
Your a (u)nique (per)spective of the world,
So (ex)press it!

♥

(Pro)cesses of Life

All is a (pro)cess,
The (pro)cesses of Life.
The rhythm of change,
Day into night.
Old & new,
Me vs you.
Who are we when we win?
Who are we when we lose?

♥

Why Did We Come Here?

We came to Earth for a reason,
For our soul to (ex)perience the seasons,
And learn it's meanings,
From these feelings we're feeling,
To (re)cognize the things we are needing.

♥

Hermetics

The Law of Mentalism

The first hermetic principle,
I wish to share is simple.
The (u)niverse is mental,
And All is (ex)periential.
All is of mind,
Seek & ye shall find.
We are all the same mankind.
Consciousness is Great Spirit,
With this (under)standing you live it.
Says the Kybalion & the three (in)itiates.

♥

The Law of Correspondence

The principle of correspondence,
Might seem like (non)sense,
(Un)til you look a little closer...
As (a)bove, so below.
Is how this law flows,
This paradox is the (un)known to known.
So (e)verything is connected.
There is no doubt.
When you follow this truth..
As within, so without.
So study the planets,
And those tiny atoms,
To find the same patterns,
Moving like Saturn.
Wisdom full to the brim,
The Great Hermes was him,
Connecting the micro & macrocosm.

♥

The Law of Vibration

There is a law (a)bout vibration,
That (re)quires some concentration,
In these teachings to (re)cognize.
The Kybalion states,
That everything vibrates,
At speeds of differing size.
A rock may seem dense,
If we sit on the fence,
Yet there is more than meets the eye.
Through a microscope we can see,
(A)toms moving at varying (de)gree,
With more space than matter...
Now what a surprise!
(De)pending on the vibration,
(De)termines the calibration,
Of our dimension,
We have been in the Third.
When we vibrate much faster,
We (ex)perience densities higher,
To (be)come as light a feather...
Of a hummingbird.

♥

The Law of Polarity

In the law of polarity,
Living this life of duality,
We've seen (op)posites as our (re)ality.
We have hot & cold.
Bought & sold.
Right & wrong.
And weak & strong.
Now in this new faculty,
All these concepts are (en)ergy.
At (op)posite ends of the scale.
To the males and females,
This wisdom's being (de)veiled.
From (an)cient Atlantic tales.
When does love (be)come hate,
On the same scale they both (re)late,
The Hermetic teachings correctly states.
When does hot become cold,
And at what point does timid become bold?
Through centuries only (in)itiates were told.
In this rhyme are keys,
To (il)luminate how we perceive..
(Op)posites are the same at differing (de)gree,
Herein lays the (u)nity of you & me.
In the (u)niversal law of polarity.

♥

The Law of Rhythm

The law of rhythm,
In motion you see 'em,
Is a rule of rise and fall.
Everything has tides,
The pendulum swings from side to side,
It's a law that governs The All.
To & fro,
Is how this life flows,
Is a key to the nature of (en)ergy.
So as we learn to use it,
And not lose ourselves in it,
we (be)come masters of extrasensory!
The wise one's knew this,
And taught it to (in)itiates,
In temples and mystery schools,
who were ready for these secrets,
(Un)locking their genius,
(A)ligning with these (u)niversal rules.

♥

The Law of Cause & Effect

The principle of cause & (e)ffect,
Is one you can easily (ac)cept,
As it's the (re)ason everything happens.
(No)thing is by chance,
This life is a dance,
To the rhythm of Eve's & Adams.
The (re)lation (be)tween (e)vents,
And the (re)sults, presents,
An (ex)perience we creatively (pro)ject.
Without a cause,
There is no (e)ffect,
Is a topic in which to (re)flect.
For if i push on this tree,
With enough (en)ergy you may see,
This principle is one to (re)spect.

♥

The Law of Gender

The principle of gender,
Is a law to (re)member,
That everything is male & female.
You may know it as sexuality,
But in all (re)ality,
Its curves and straight lines of (en)ergy.
Men are half women,
And women are half Men,
Like two five's (e)qualling ten.
More than that,
This (U)niverse is in fact,
A manifestation of this principle.

♥

(An)tiquity

Brothers & Sisters

Brothers & Sisters,
Silently whisper,
(An)cient scriptures we're told,
Brothers & Sisters,
Human figures,
our (an)cestors of old.
Brothers & Sisters,
Coming to gather,
In (u)nity we hold.
Brothers & Sisters,
It is now time,
To clear up the mould.
Brothers & Sisters,
we're all winners,
why be bitter & cold?
Brothers & Sisters
we are all victors,
As old ways wither & fold.

♥

The Hero's Journey

Many types of theology,
Are concealed in mythology.
I (in)vite you to (in)vestigate.
If you look in old stories,
The lead character,
And their glories,
Joseph Campbell (pro)claimed to state.
It's called the hero's journey,
This life we are living,
So be (pre)pared,
To look with new eyes.
For there are great mysteries,
In these lives that we lead,
So (in)vestigate and you might be surprised!

♥

way out west

way out west,
(A)long (En)gland's green fields,
Lay lands of old stories,
In swords & shields.
Mysterious stone circles,
Hidden deep within moors,
Tell stories of humankind,
And the building of tors.
Castles of King Arthur,
(Re)main to (re)mind us all,
The legend of (Ex)calibur,
And giants 20ft tall.
Merlin the magician,
Weaving spells of forgotten falls,
(U)pon these crystal hills,
In a place called Cornwall.

♥

His-story

Now let's talk about his-story.
What we've been told is just one story,
Said by the winners of every war.
To keep their control,
They have told what they've told,
With (a)cademics on the payroll.
I (in)vite you to look for yourselves,
At the (e)vidence on (in)ternet shelves.
That our story is way much older.
Check out the Sphinx,
And Robert Schoch's links,
About the (e)rosion of limestone by water.
This is a factuality,
A science of geology,
(Ex)amining rocks,
Not (E)gyptology.
So when Schoch's facts suggests,
His dating is not a guess,
It throws a question to the age of humanity...
Now for Gobekli Tepe,
(Dis)covered for many (de)cades,
Who's age is still a mystery.
Some say 10,000,
Others say 20,000,
Either which it [re]writes our story.
So i feel we can (a)gree,
There is more than we can see,
(A)bout our past & our (an)cient archaeology.

♥

Footsteps & Shoulders

The story continues,
On the highway of human history,
Our home Pachamama,
Is filled with (an)cient mysteries.
In the garden of (re)membrance,
Flowers the great (a)wakening,
This forgotten path,
We are all participating in.
Following the footsteps of legends,
Uncovering the shoulders of giants,
Honouring the past,
And forgiving the tyrants.
Live life in love,
Is what we're asking of you,
As we walk each other home,
To a place you (al)ways knew.

♥

Syncretism

When you take time to listen,
To the wisdom of syncretism,
You'll see more clearly than you ever have before.
Joining every (re)ligion,
Theology & world vision,
It (u)nites all stories & more!
For it (re)lates to our Sun,
Mohamed, Krishna & Ra are one,
Jesus is the Heart & our core.
So drop the (i)deology & stand back,
For it's all in the zodiac,
There need no division or separation (an)ymore.
The 12 signs of the constellations,
Are the 12 (dis)ciples in (re)velations,
Arthur's round table knights in folklore.
The seasonal movements of our star,
(Re)flect what's going on in our avatar,
This body is God's temple to (ex)plore...
Now you see the big picture,
And how it's written in scripture,
So look for syncretism in your local bookstore!

♥

Question what to Believe

Stars of wonder,
In the great beyond,
Hold mysteries so strange,
I find myself ponder.
What i do know,
Is there is light up there,
That seems to suggest,
Some kind of order.
Everything else,
Is stuff we've been sold,
The shapes & the sizes,
And (dis)tances told.
In the age of (in)formation,
Fed to us by machines,
I choose to question,
What we've been fed to believe.

♥

Magic Spelling

These words, Symbols & Signs

These words im sharing,
Are simply labels,
To (ex)press myself in rhyme.
Which help me convey,
What i wish to say,
Like fiction,
They are the product of mind.
The language i use,
To speak my trooth,
(un)tethers the (un)conscious (de)sign.
For now we're luminated,
The collective they've dictated,
Through these words & symbols & signs.
So what's the meaning of a label,
When written in a fable?
You must read between the lines.
To uncover the mystery,
Of the word & his-story,
To unlock the matrix & the (il)lusion of time.

♥

Words of wisdom

In the rivers of (re)membering,
The current of math,
Flows the trooth of life,
We must never forget.
Pure language to (ex)press,
The love of this path,
In my dream i (re)write,
Romeo & Juliet.
Moving like water
To be fluid & free,
Playing with form,
Creating timeless silhouettes.
Share these words of wisdom,
Whoever you may be,
For these rhymes are magic spells,
Constructed with love & the (al)phabet!

♥

Fiction To Fact

You aint (pro)gramming me,
I'm (pro)gramming you.
I see through the veil,
And you can too.
These poison (pre)fixes,
Are (de)liberate (re)mixes,
of our language,
To keep us confused.
So by dropping the act,
from fiction to fact,
And (a)voiding the traps,
of fraudulent (in)come tax,
To write parse syntax contracts.

♥

If You Have The Eyes To See

If you have the eyes to see,
You'll see a beautiful man in me,
One who lives his life,
Full of joy & (em)pathy.
If you have the eyes to see,
You'll see a courageous side me,
One who follows his heart,
In a tide of fear & (un)certainty.
If you have the eyes to see,
You'll see a very different me,
One who shines a light so bright,
The whole world can see.
If you have the eyes to see,
You'll see a surprising side of me,
One who's masters the art,
Of magic & wizardry...
If you have the eyes to see,
You'll see an (an)gel in me,
One who writes a sentence,
As pure as maths can be...
If you have the eyes to see,
You'll see a legend in me,
One who cracks the code,
Of the word & literacy.
And if you have the eyes to see,
You'll see a mighty king in me,
One who frees the people,
From modern slavery.

♥

(In)ner Library

(I)magine yourself as a library,
That's (in)finitely big in size,
With all of life's knowledge,
For you to see with your eyes.
This library contains your treasure,
That's in your (in)terests to find,
This is your (in)ner library,
With keys that help you be kind.
These keys unlock doors to yesterdays past,
Karmically untied to be free.
Now you know where to look,
To find the right book,
In the (a)kashic library..
Of you & me.

♥

The Magic of A Roundabout.

I'll give you a clue..
Maybe a riddle or two,
(A)bout the magic of a roundabout.
How magicians journal,
Creates magic we make verbal..
That's had us going (a)round & round in circles.
There's something (a)bout a roundabout,
That everybody needs to know.
If you continue as you are,
Means (a)round & round you go.
When you master the riddle,
You know the spelling's been fiddled.
Its not (a)bout turning right,
Its (a)bout learning to read & write,
So we can know & stand up for our rites...
(A)right..
All write!

♥

What Is A (De)finition.

what is a (de)finition,
when (de)finition means..
No/de-finition?
Is a matter i wish to (pre)sent.
What's happened to our language,
That causes such negation of (an)guish?
It's bad spelling & i do not consent.
So what is a (de)finition,
In a matter of law..
Is it matter of fiction,
Or is it a matter of fact..
Is it a this or that?

♥

To write (A)bout..

When we know what is right or wrong,
(A)bout how we write (a)bout,
And why we write (a)bout (a)bout.
It's a matter of serendipity,
To free us of this (il)literacy,
And bring down this demon-ocracy.

♥

(Ne)gation

I stumbled on a mystery,
(A)bout the word & his-story,
(A)round the campfire with you last night.
When you see the (ne)gation,
It causes a (re)velation,
That changes your destiny.

♥

I AM-The One

I wrote every word,
Thats ever been written,
witch means..
I've written every word,
That one's ever wrote.

I sang every song,
That's ever been sung,
witch means..
I've sung every song,
That one's ever sung.

I am every man,
That's ever been born,
And...

I am every woman,
That's ever been scorn.

I am everything,
one's ever been,
And..
I AM-The One,
who is creating this dream.

♥

For The Claim of The Life

Do ye know (a)bout the C'est tu que vie?
It's a law that says ye dead...
or lost at sea.
We lost control to pirates,
of our common law lands,
To maritime (ad)miralty.
So when ye stand up in court,
And shout ye name out forth,
It's not an (ad)visable place to be..
You've just docked your vessel,
In a dock in foreign territory.
It's a trick..
It's a trap,
It's a total fraud.
(Ig)nore their letters,
Don't walk through those doors.
Get off their ships,
Get out of the seas,
Vacate their river banks,
And fake currencies.
I spell ye some great (ad)vice,
Stand up for ye rites,
By learning to read & write,
For the claim of the CLAIM-OF-LIFE.

♥

Etymology

To know (et)ymology,
You may need to etymology etymology,
To know the origin of the word.
It's more than just spelling,
It's a tale they're telling,
It's a script they wrote..
Have you heard?
A story in first person,
Second person,
And third.
Do you know your conjunctions, (ad)jectives & verbs...
And (pre)fixes, (pro)nouns and (ad)verbs?
We must learn to read & write,
For their spelling is a curse,
A (ne)gation of Life..
Rise up before it gets worse!
We can write our own story,
Full of passion & glory,
In (re)verence to Life..
And all we are worth.

♥

1+2=3=Me+You=we

What is 1+2=3?
It's the (u)nity in me - which is 1,
The duality in you - that makes 2,
(E)quals the trinity in we - that makes 3.
Can you see?
We're all number (en)coded with mastery!
I am you,
You are me,
We are the seeds..
That create the (e)ternal triangles of trinity.
Can you see?
We're all children & patterns of geometry.
So what's a double in trinity?
Is a 6 i call (in)finity.
Trust me..
This math leads to grand (e)piphanies.
Now let's add 3+6=9.
In these times tables you will find,
A Heavenly (de)sign,
I call in-fin-trinity.
Can you see a pattern (a)lign,
with the never changing 9?
This 9 (re)peats (re)peatedly,
3 & 6 (os)cilate continually,..
When you study numerology,
You see the divinity,
of Life & all humanity....

Now lets reverse the sum..

$$3-2=1,$$

Maths is who you are,

You are the one,

who created this all for fun.

The Heavens,

The Earth..

And The Golden Sun.

This maths is a map of the stars,

(Re)member you're a map of an (an)cient past,

You're a map to heal all of your scars.

That's what You are..

You're a galactic avatar.

So the 3 that's in we,

Is the 2 that's in you,

Is the 1 that's in me,

Can you see?

This is a rhythmical numerical symphony..

So The one in me,

Makes peace with you plus two,

Equals three we are free,

Together we live forever in trigonometry.

♥

The wisdom of The word

The wisdom of the word,
Is mysterious & magical.
It is a master key,
which manifests our lives,
In hell or harmony.

♥

The Secret In Numbers

If you knew,
what numbers...
1 to 9 can do,
I promise you,
You'll believe it too.
More than that,
As a matter of fact,
I can do it,
And so can you!
In this code are secrets,
That now we are ready to see.
And when we know it...
In the body,
Its forever (im)mortality!

♥

Path of Least Resistance

Why not just (ac)cept it,
You're God..
Or whatever name you call it.
It is simply a word,
Like your name,
Or and (adj)ective,
Or a verb.
Now is the time to see it,
You're The Creator,
Of this whole (ex)istence.
You are all people's,
And all planets...
You're even the (dis)tance!
You ask..
How can that be?
I ask..
Who is that which sees?
Now follow this path of least (re)sistance.

♥

The Poet Be-Comes The Poem

There's something poetic (a)bout the ways of the world,
And the language to (de)scribe it.
when i find it,
It's very (re)vealing,
And full of (i)ronic surprises.
Every word can be (ob)served,
To find a deeper meaning,
A (per)fect (re)flection,
An (em)bodied moment,
The poet be-comes the poem.

♥

#

Who's Scribbled The Script?

Who's been writing our story?
This is the land of trooth & glory.
What scribe has scribbled these scripts?
Why's everything been flipped?
Whoever's sitting in the saddle,
Has taught us bible bibble babble.
You must do your (re)search,
To vacate the Babylonian church.
It's Jacob's ladder we've got to climb,
And leave those two pillars (be)hind.
Saturn will show us the way,
In the Aquarian Age today,
Where the power of money,
Is drowned in milk & honey.

♥

The Clues To Get Out Of This Mess

I write these lines,
with a rhythm in mind,
In a way i feel them (ex)pressed.
I write these rhymes,
In a riddle of a kind,
To help your mind (de)stress.
I write these words,
In the trust you will find,
The clues to get out of this mess.
I write these signs,
In curves & straight lines,
with this knowledge you can pass the test.

♥

Linguistic Prison

How long will it be,
Til you rise up and see,
This life for you and me.
We are (e)ternally living.
Collapsing this old matrix system,
Breaking free from this linguistic prison.

♥

New Earth

Daughters & Sons

Through these poems i'm making,

From the heart they came flowing,
Into (ex)istance,
To read.
Straight from The Source,
Through a hand,
of course.
It's a pleasure, a service and a deed.
It's made to (in)spire,
To (ig)nite the fire,
For this New Earth to transpire!
So our daughters & sons
Can stay (in-no)cent and fun,
On Earth this day,
We be-come one.

♥

Our Playground

I was blind,

Now i can see,
I make you a finder,
Just like me.

I was lost,
Now I've found.
The New Earth,
Is our playground.

Keep your eyes open,
So you can see,
A rainbow over stonehenge,
To know that you are free.

♥

Walk With Me

I am (e)ternally living,
A master being of light.
A humble servant of God,
A shining white knight.
(Act)ions of pure (in)tention,
(Act)ivations of trooth.
An (an)gel from Heaven,
For I Am the proof.
Walk with me,
To the garden of (E)den,
To know you are home,
In the New Earth we are seeding.

♥

(In)ner Guru

There is no (e)scaping,
This mass (a)wakening,
That we have all come here to witness.
The event we've been hearing,
Is here if we are clearing,
This conditioning we didn't know was (a)miss.
It takes some brave (in)vestigating,
In shadows we're navigating,
This fear of the (a)byss.
So drop all your worries,
And move out of Surrey
To find your (in)ner guru..
Which is your heart & your bliss.

♥

The Great Uplifting

The great uplifting,
we are all participating in,
Is a mysterious and magical thing.
It requires a transformation,
To (em)body the (re)velations,
That creates the change you came here to sing.
So when you jump on the rollercoaster,
With no idea which way it'll throw ya,
Know it's the high road,
The path of a King.
And just so you know,
This life may seem slow,
Yet this (a)scension is happening right now.
So i suggest you take note,
Of this book that i wrote,
Or get a copy of the wisdom of the Tao.

♥

Transformational Force

On the 11th of August,
when you heard that chorus,
I magically played to you.
To show you what's possible,
That this force is unstoppable.
Transforming this Earth (a)new.

♥

(In)tervention

This is an (in)tervention,
Shrouded in mystery.
Working undercover,
(Re)writing our story.
Swallow your pride,
And open your eyes.
For a new day is coming..
Full of love,
That will make You cry.

♥

I AM

I Am a Life hacker.
Soul shaker.
Terraforming..
Freedom paver.

I Am a tantric lover.
Spectrum of colour.
Seed sowing..
Story teller.

I am the singularity,
of the (U)nity.
The polarity,
In the duality,
Singing rhymes to (re)mind humanity.
A light to inner cities.
To change the course of society.

I Am a DJ spinner.
Lyrical writer.
(Re)negade master,
Galvanizing..
Chemical Brother.

I Am a Mother lovin'
Sweet talkin'
Shamanic walkin'
Father & Son..
The one.

♥

Where We Go One We Go All

Where we go one,
we go all.
What's (e)ternally living,
Is (in)side us all.

Where we go one,
we go all.
In our darkest shadows,
In those times we fall.

Where we go one,
we go all.
(Ex)posing the lies,
Of the deep state cabal.

Where we go one,
we go all.
Our brothers & sisters
Standing tall.

Where we go one,
we go all.
(Re)member the plan,
You (an)swered the call.

Where we go one,
we go all.
Human beings,
Free from rule...

Where we go one,
we go all.
The trooth of life,
And a bundance for all.

Where we go one,
we go all.
Consciously living,
In magic & miracles.

♥

Family

Divine (or)der

(on)ce (u)pon a time,
we came together to make a plan,
To (u)nite on a journey we didn't (under)stand.
If we knew what would happen,
It may have changed our direction,
For there is a divine (or)der,
And we're (a)ligned with..
Its perfection.

♥

8.8.8.

The (in)finite number 8,

For me i (re)late,
To the Lion's Gate,
Sirius magic to (under)take.
This connection was fate,
(O)pening a stargate,
The significance so great,
We came to co-create.
(U)nion on a plate,
With love & bliss as the bait,
Lifetimes to wait,
Not a second too late,
For this love story i narrate,
The coming to-gather of Soulmates,
In divine love to (pro)create,
Children of light who radiate,
New Earth traits,
(In)spiring you to cultivate,
(Ex)periences to celebrate,
A world we liberate.
In rhyme i translate,
The majestic date,
Of 8.8.8.

♥

The Great (Ad)venture

The great (ad)venture,
Letting go of the past,
Moving forward,
Life changing so fast.
New (be)ginnings,
Home by the sea,
A beautiful family,
(E)ternally free.
Colour lit sunset,
Caressing my face,
(In)nocent children,
Are a wondrous grace.
Ready to fly,
My soul is ready,
Consciousness rising,
Feeling so steady.
Flowers in light,
Free as a bird,
(En)lightenment is here,
I give you my word.

♥

Can You See?

Can you see the wonder & magic of life,
In a world with so much beauty?
Can you see the wonder & magic of life,
In a world with so much cruelty?
Can you see the wonder & magic of life,
In perfect divine (or)der?
I can see the wonder & magic in life,
In the eyes of our two daughters.

♥

My Family of Magic & Wonder

We were meant to come together.
It had to be us.
You & i..
No other.
With the power of a tornado,
Riding through Mexico.
Uma chose you as her Mother.
The white wizard (de)scended,
From the stars reunited,
The two of us as twin lovers.
Life is taking me away,
With Gaia's (ar)rival i say..
I will (re)turn to see you all grow older.
My Love and tears are real.
With this (un)conditional heart i feel..
My Family of magic & wonder.

♥

Where Do We Go From Here?

Where do we go from here?
I trust we know,
I hope it so,
Letting go of the perception of fear.
I feel your pain,
I am able to see,
Our beautiful family's needs,
In this cold November rain.
How do things change,
For us to live free,
In one heart you & me,
When (no)thing stays the same.
The future is a mystery,
So let's find the solutions,
Letting go of conclusions,
(Ac)cepting our choices as our-story.
So let's live in the (pre)sent,
And the gifts it brings,
In whatever way Life sing's,
'Cause it's our dream to (re)invent.

♥

The Time Has Come

The time has come,
For us to part,
My sweet dear girls,
It breaks my heart.
To leave you (on)ce,
was so much pain,
And now we have to face it again.
I know one day,
we will have our time,
To tell our story,
And heal this crime.
I will always love you,
You both have to know,
And i know one day,
You will feel it so.
And when that day comes,
There's a pot of gold,
waiting for you,
where our trooths be told.

♥

My Babies I Love You

My babies i'm sorry im i'm not with you,
Through this part of your Life your you're going through.
I know it's not easy,
To feel that you need me,
This (ab)sence will be of some value.
So trust why i am away,
I feel your pain & dismay
'Cause we are one..
My babies i love you.

♥

Sweet Uma & Gaia

Why were things the way they were,
when i left you in Mexico?
I came to reconnect with you,
Until i was told to go.
It broke my heart to leave that way,
i had so much i wanted to say..
Everything will be ok.
We will meet again,
I know this so,
For life has a way it wants to flow,
Sweet Uma & Gaia,
I love you both.
You will know this trooth,
When your ready to know,
Remember...
Life always gives us what we need to grow.

♥

Oh Grief

Oh grief...
Bless you for your presence,
Sometimes you feel like a sentence,
That doesn't ever want to end.
It comes from a place,
of love i call grace,
A necessary evil that leads to despair.
Honor the separation,
And feelings of desperation,
That this pain is part of the game
Lord give me the strength,
with all these tears i've spent,
To see it's a process of love & sorrow.
I thank you for these lessons,
of grief & acceptance,
So a wise Man can grow & let go.

♥

Goodbye Sadness

I went back to the woods i know,
To say goodbye to who i used to be.
Goodbye to the sadness,
And all of that madness,
Giving myself (pe)mission to be happy and free.
Alone with the fire,
Gave me time to (en)quire,
What it is my heart wants to sing.
And now that i know,
I trust in myself to grow,
And fly with these new found wings.

♥

Dear Tara

At the next plant ceremony,
I'm sure you will agree,
It will have me beaming at you,
And you beaming at me.
Or maybe its LSD,
Whatever it will be,
Will have me beaming at you,
And you beaming at me.
If this is the case,
Why are we in this place,
Of denying this cosmic grace?
I have what it takes,
To (a)bundantly generate,
A life fit for a Queen.
Happy & free,
In our wildest dreams,
As a model of a new Earth family.
We must first learn our lessons,
Of pain & separation,
To understand what we were fighting for.
And maybe then we can open,
Past what was broken,
To new versions of ourselves to explore.

♥

Inspiration Co-creation

What do these poems (in)spire in you,
I would love you to (ex)press,
Whatever your heart suggests,
In any way to (im)press,
The trooths that I'm sharing with you.
Paint what you see,
or build my (e)piphany.
However it is,
Do whatever you do,
As an (in)spiration,
From me to you.

♥

Printed in Great Britain
by Amazon